(Is this the way to)

Words and m

4

When the day is dawn- / -ing on a Te- xas Sun - day morn - ing, how I long to be____ there / with Ma- rie who's wait- / -ing for me____ there.

ba ba da ba bow

Ev -'ry lone - ly ci - ty

Ev -'ry lone - ly ci - ty

43 S. A.

MEN cry-ing o - ver A - ma-ril - lo and sweet Ma-rie who waits___ for me.

47 *ff*

Sha la la la la___ la la la sha la la la la___ la la la

51 **2nd time to Coda** (p. 9)

sha la la la la___ la la la and Ma-rie who waits_ for me.

2nd time to Coda (p. 9)

55 S.

ding - a - ding dong.

A.

There's a church bell ring - ing, hear the song of joy_

mf

D. S. 𝄋 (p. 5) **al** 𝄌 (p. 7) **poi al Coda** 𝄌 **CODA**

D. S. 𝄋 (p. 5) **al** 𝄌 (p. 7) **poi al Coda** 𝄌 **CODA**

la la la   sha la la   la la____ la la la

and Ma-rie   who waits__ for me.   ah_____

bap   bap!

Dream a little dream of me

Words and music by Willy Schwandt, Fabian Andre and Gus Kahn
arr. Alexander L'Estrange

12

Can't take my eyes off you

Words and music by Bob Crewe and Bob Gaudio
arr. Alexander L'Estrange

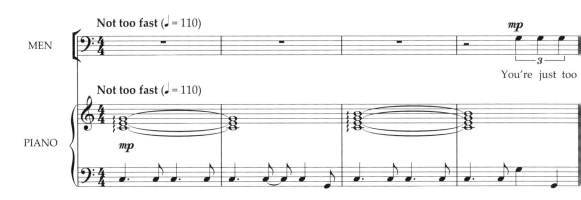

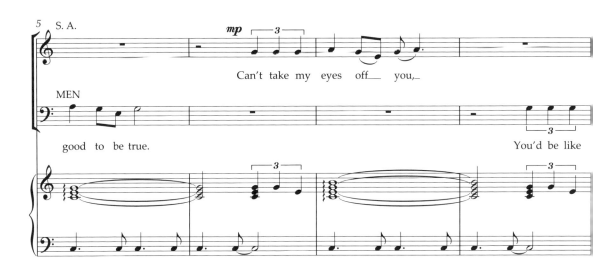

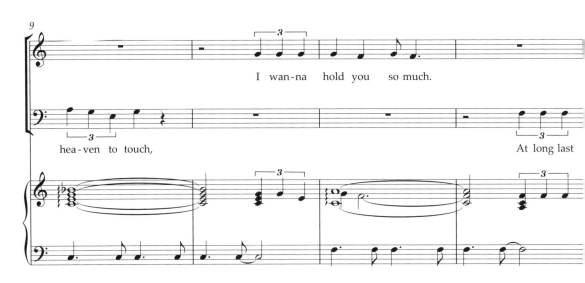